Windmi

Althea and Edward Parker
Illustrations by Peter Bailey

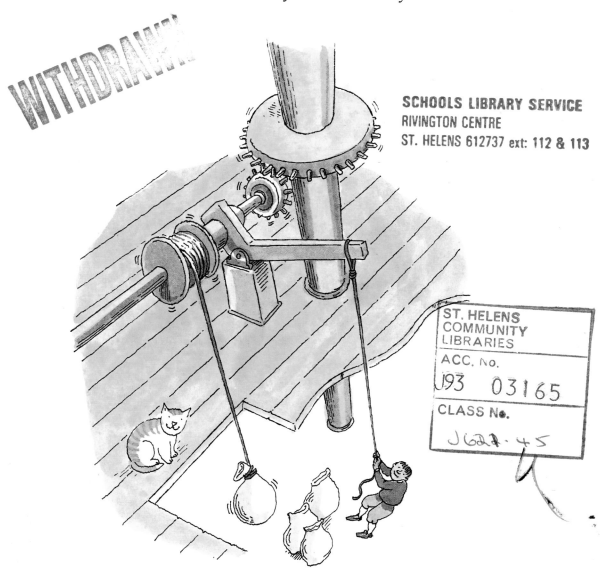

A&C Black · London

First published 1992
A & C Black (Publishers) Limited
35 Bedford Row, London, WC1R 4JH

ISBN 0-7136-3532-0

A CIP catalogue record for this book is
available from the British Library

Acknowledgements

Edited by Barbara Taylor
Photographs by: Butser Ancient Farm
page 4; Denny Plowman, Green's Mill, Nottingham
pages 13, 14, 16, 23, 27; Avoncroft Museum of
Buildings, Bromsgrove, Worcestershire pages
10, 20; PowerGen page 31.

The authors would like to thank the
people at Green's Mill, Nottingham
and Downfield Mill, Soham for their
invaluable help and advice during
the preparation of this book.

Filmset by Rowland Phototypesetting
Printed and bound in Italy by L.E.G.O. Spa.

Contents

From corn to flour

Rye

Oats

The first windmills were built probably more than a thousand years ago, and windmills are still used today to grind corn, pump water and drain flooded land. The ideas behind windmills are also being used in wind turbines to generate electricity.

Wheat

Windmills were invented to solve a problem: how could people grind enough corn to make the flour needed for baking bread?

Many hundreds of years ago, corn was ground by hand. This was done either by thumping the corn with a wooden stake, or by grinding it between two stones. These methods were slow, hard work and only made small amounts of flour at a time.

Barley

The grain from all these plants can be called corn.

You would be hungry by the time you had crushed enough grain in this mortar to make a loaf of bread.

The grains were put on to the bottom stone, called the quern, and the top stone was pushed round, crushing or grinding the grain between the two stones.

Horse mill

Much more flour could be made using large and heavy stones but these needed a gang of people or horses or oxen to turn them. The millstones were designed so that the grain could be fed through the top stone on to the bottom one. As the meal was ground, it trickled out through grooves in the stones.

This way, the stones could be kept grinding without stopping every few minutes to add more corn. It produced a lot more flour, but it was still very hard work, and the animals also needed time off for food and rest.

Millstone

Power for mills

Water was first used to power millstones in Ancient Greece thousands of years ago. The watermill had a wooden wheel with paddles attached to it. It had to be built next to a river or stream. The paddles were turned by the flowing water, and as the wheel turned, it turned the millstones.

Watermills were much faster than horse mills but were very expensive to build. Only rich landowners or religious institutions could afford them, and they charged a lot of money to grind other people's corn. As the population grew, more and more people wanted flour so a way of working the mills more cheaply had to be found. This was long before electricity or steam engines had been invented.

An early watermill

The wind was a powerful source of energy which was already being used to drive sailing boats. People realized that this energy could also be used to turn a millstone. Early records tell of a farmer in Persia (modern-day Iran) building a windmill to grind his corn in AD 644.

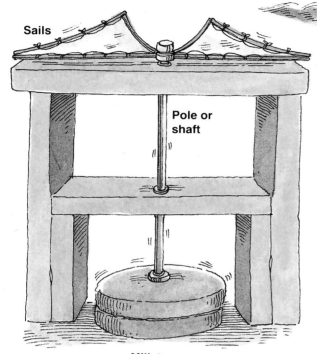

Sails

Pole or shaft

Millstones

There were lots of experiments with wind sails before a working machine capable of turning a millstone was built. The earliest windmill had horizontal sails and might have looked something like this picture.

The sails were on a shaft, and when the wind blew the sails, the shaft turned the millstone at the bottom. This didn't work very well because the sails turned slowly in the wind and the millstone didn't go round fast enough to make fine flour.

MUSICAL WINDMILL

In the Second Century AD, a Greek scientist named Hero invented an organ powered by a windmill.

Later mills had upright sails attached to a shaft. When the wind blew the sails round, they turned the windshaft. A big wheel – called the brake wheel – was fixed to the windshaft. This brake wheel had pegs, or teeth, which fitted into the teeth on a small wheel called a wallower. The wallower was fixed to the main shaft, which turned the millstone. When the big wheel turned, it drove the small wheel round. Each turn of the big wheel made the small wheel turn several times, so the main shaft turned faster than the windshaft.

To make the millstone go even faster, more toothed wheels or gear wheels were added at the bottom of the main shaft, as you can see on the next page.

Brake wheel

Wallower

The pegs on the brake wheel and the wallower fit together as they turn.

WINDMILL CATAPULTS

Windmills may have been used as catapults to hurl beehives at a castle during a siege.

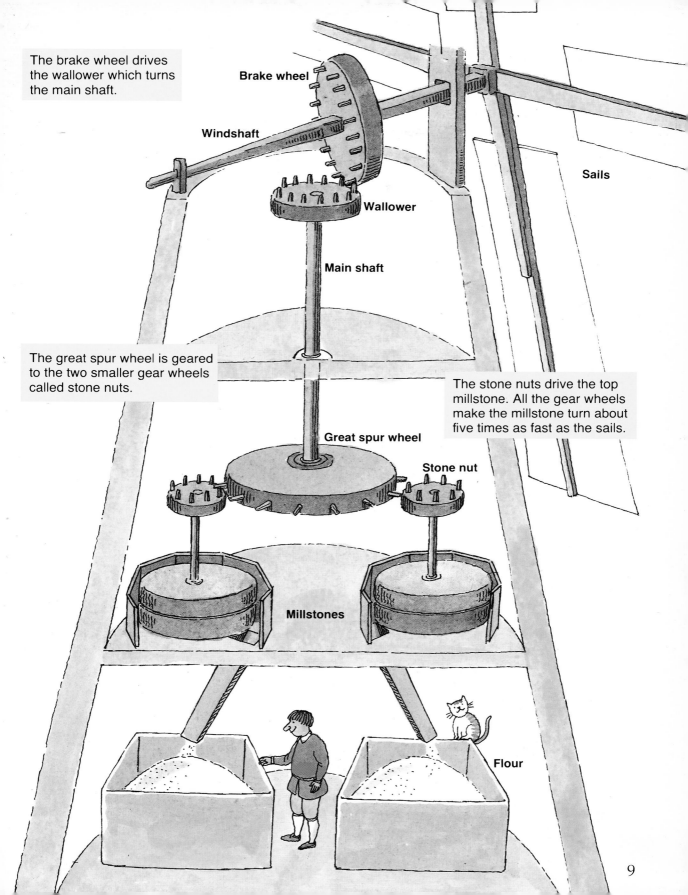

The brake wheel drives the wallower which turns the main shaft.

Brake wheel

Windshaft

Sails

Wallower

Main shaft

The great spur wheel is geared to the two smaller gear wheels called stone nuts.

The stone nuts drive the top millstone. All the gear wheels make the millstone turn about five times as fast as the sails.

Great spur wheel

Stone nut

Millstones

Flour

9

Post mills

The early windmills rested on a huge upright post, so they were called post mills. The post rested on two cross posts. These cross posts rested on, or were buried in, the ground. After a time, people found that the cross posts rotted in the damp soil so they raised them above the ground, resting them on brick or stone piers.

The roundhouse was added to protect the cross posts from the weather. It was also useful for storing the grain and flour.

To keep the sails facing the wind, the miller swung the whole building round the central post. He pushed on a large beam called the tailpole, which was attached to the back of the mill.

It was heavy work, and sometimes mills were blown over because the miller couldn't turn the mill in time. To make it easier, a wheel was fitted to the tailpole and a paved path, or rail track, was laid around the mill. Sometimes a horse was used to pull the heavy mill around.

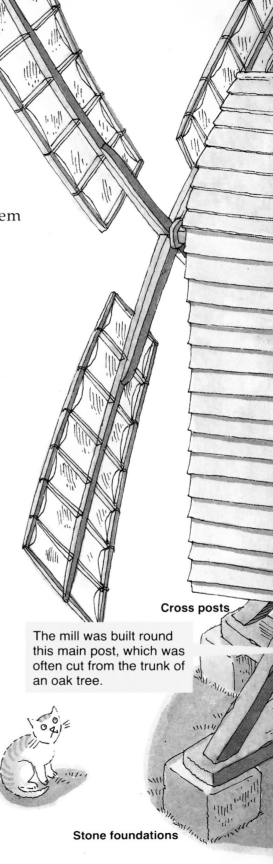

Cross posts

The mill was built round this main post, which was often cut from the trunk of an oak tree.

Stone foundations

10

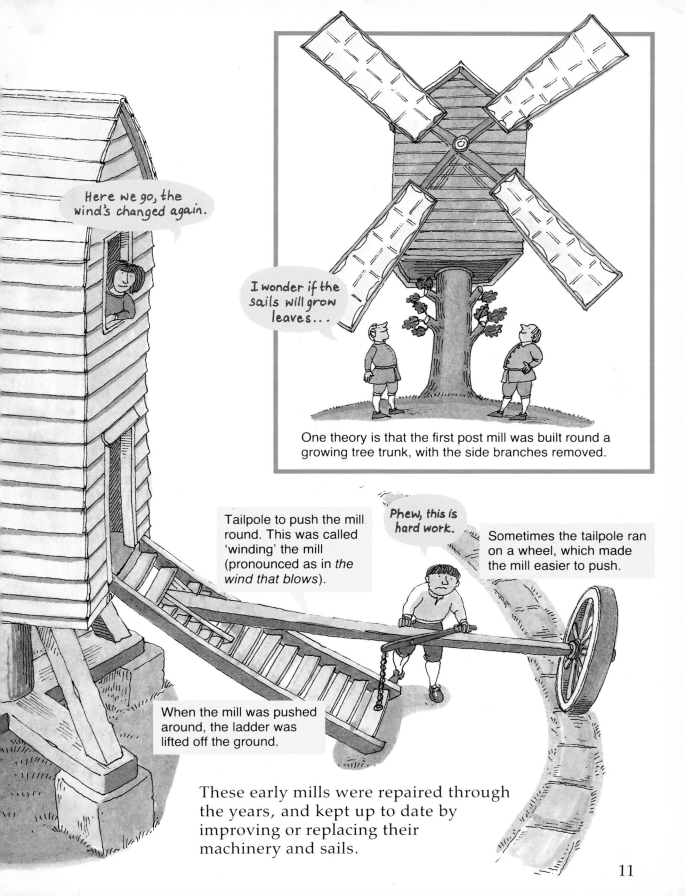

Here we go, the wind's changed again.

I wonder if the sails will grow leaves...

One theory is that the first post mill was built round a growing tree trunk, with the side branches removed.

Tailpole to push the mill round. This was called 'winding' the mill (pronounced as in *the wind that blows*).

Phew, this is hard work.

Sometimes the tailpole ran on a wheel, which made the mill easier to push.

When the mill was pushed around, the ladder was lifted off the ground.

These early mills were repaired through the years, and kept up to date by improving or replacing their machinery and sails.

11

Smock and tower mills

Later, various methods of 'winding' the mill automatically were tried. The most successful designs started by having the sails and windshaft mounted in a cap at the top of the mill. This cap turned around the top of the mill building on something like a circular railway track. Now it was not necessary to move the whole mill when the wind changed.

Cap

The windshaft, with its sails, was mounted in this cap. When the wind changed direction, the cap turned on a rail to 'wind' the sails. The rest of the mill didn't move.

That fantail's a clever invention – saves a lot of work.

Main sails

That mill looks just like your smock George.

Smock mills got their name because they looked like the smocks worn by country workers of the day. Smock mills usually had eight sides.

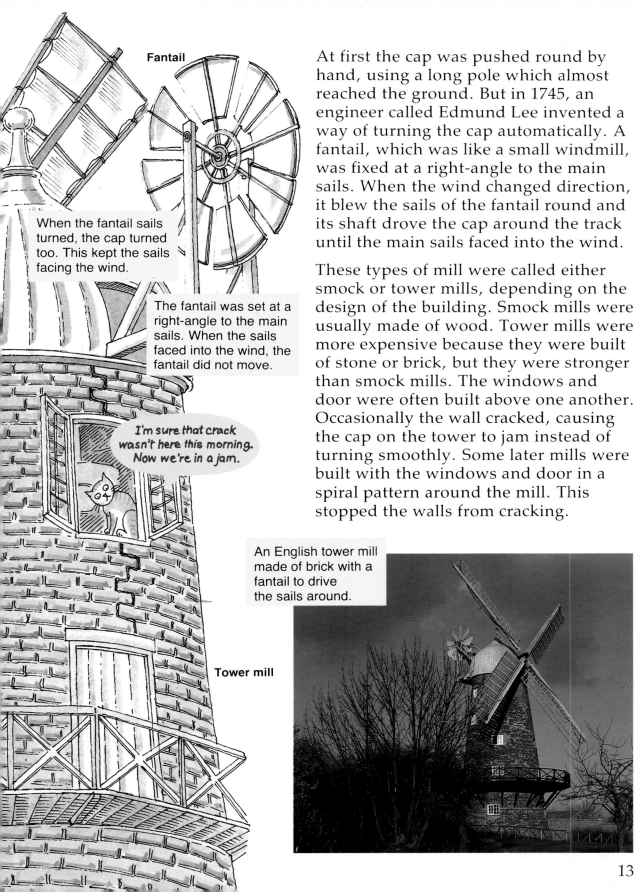

Fantail

When the fantail sails turned, the cap turned too. This kept the sails facing the wind.

The fantail was set at a right-angle to the main sails. When the sails faced into the wind, the fantail did not move.

I'm sure that crack wasn't here this morning. Now we're in a jam.

Tower mill

An English tower mill made of brick with a fantail to drive the sails around.

At first the cap was pushed round by hand, using a long pole which almost reached the ground. But in 1745, an engineer called Edmund Lee invented a way of turning the cap automatically. A fantail, which was like a small windmill, was fixed at a right-angle to the main sails. When the wind changed direction, it blew the sails of the fantail round and its shaft drove the cap around the track until the main sails faced into the wind.

These types of mill were called either smock or tower mills, depending on the design of the building. Smock mills were usually made of wood. Tower mills were more expensive because they were built of stone or brick, but they were stronger than smock mills. The windows and door were often built above one another. Occasionally the wall cracked, causing the cap on the tower to jam instead of turning smoothly. Some later mills were built with the windows and door in a spiral pattern around the mill. This stopped the walls from cracking.

Sails

Most of the early mills were short, so that the miller could reach the sails to adjust them. However, mills built amongst trees or buildings had to be taller to catch the wind. These mills had a platform round them so that the miller could still reach the sails.

The early 'common sails' were made of a wooden frame with canvas laced to it. When the wind blew fiercely, the miller had to quickly reduce the amount of canvas, by rolling it up and tying it down. If this was not done in time, the sails could spin so fast they might be ripped from the building.

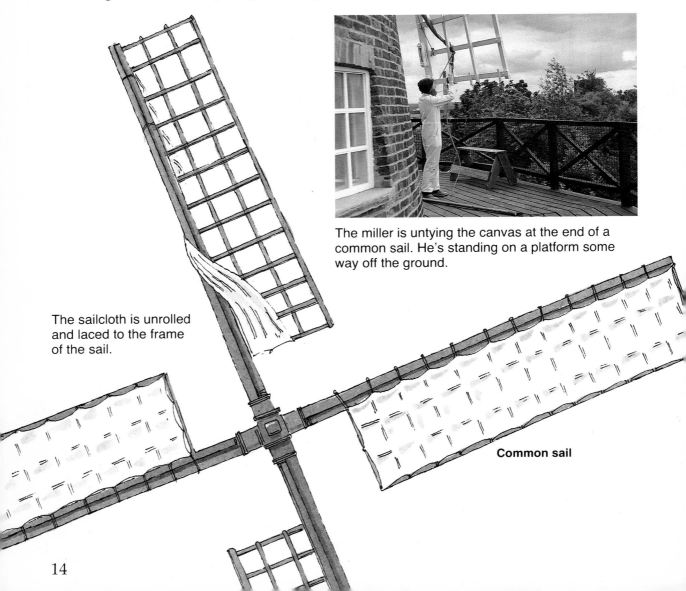

The miller is untying the canvas at the end of a common sail. He's standing on a platform some way off the ground.

The sailcloth is unrolled and laced to the frame of the sail.

Common sail

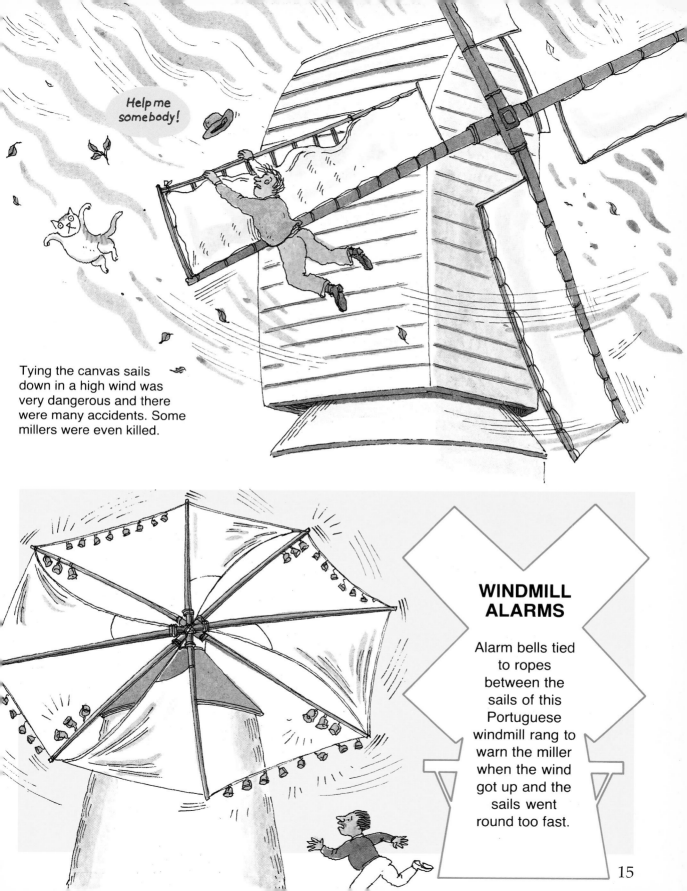

Help me somebody!

Tying the canvas sails down in a high wind was very dangerous and there were many accidents. Some millers were even killed.

WINDMILL ALARMS

Alarm bells tied to ropes between the sails of this Portuguese windmill rang to warn the miller when the wind got up and the sails went round too fast.

15

In 1772, an engineer called Andrew Meikle designed sails called 'spring sails' which were much safer and easier to adjust. They had two rows of hinged shutters, like the slats of a louvre or sunblind. Each slat acted like a small sail. The slats were connected together so their angle could be altered by turning a lever. Each sail had to be adjusted separately, but it was much quicker and safer than trying to tie down canvas. Spring sails were not as powerful as common sails though, so millers sometimes compromised by having two of each.

The mill has to be stopped to adjust spring sails. If the wind starts to blow strongly, the slats can be opened by turning a lever. This lets some wind blow through the sails, so they don't turn too fast.

Spring sail

In a light wind, the slats are closed, and the wind pushes against the sail to turn it.

The wind is getting up, I'll open the slats.

Spring

Slats

Common sail

Each slat is made of canvas, with a wooden frame, and painted with white lead to stop the canvas from rotting.

In about 1800, William Cubitt invented 'patent sails'. These were similar to 'spring sails' but they could be adjusted without stopping the sails. Taller mills could now be built. Some of the older smock mills and tower mills had bricks added to their bases to make them taller.

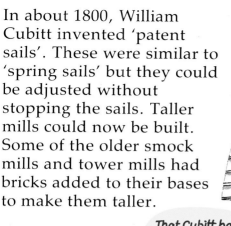

Patent sail

That Cubitt had some good ideas. I wish I'd thought of this years ago.

Patent sails could sometimes be adjusted from inside the mill.

Different numbers of sails were tried to see which worked best. Extra sails gave the mill more grinding power, but too many slowed things down again. With even numbers of sails it was easy to take off the opposite sail if one was damaged. Mills with four sails remained the most common as they could be run on two sails while repairs were made.

Grinding the corn

The grain had to be fed into the machinery at the top of the mill. Hauling the grain up was hard work, so sack hoists were designed which used the power from the main shaft to drive a chain drum, rather like a bucket hoist in a water well.

Main shaft

Sack of grain

That's better!

This is heavy work, I'm exhausted.

This sack hoist makes the miller's life easier.

The grain was poured through a sieve into a square grain bin which fed the hoppers. Grain trickled down to a trough called the 'shoe' which rested on the casing or the top millstone, called the 'runner stone'. When the runner stone turned, it shook the shoe and the grain fell into the 'eye' of the stone.

The faster the wind blew, the faster the runner stone turned, and the faster the shoe shook the grain out. The grain fell between the stones and was crushed into meal.

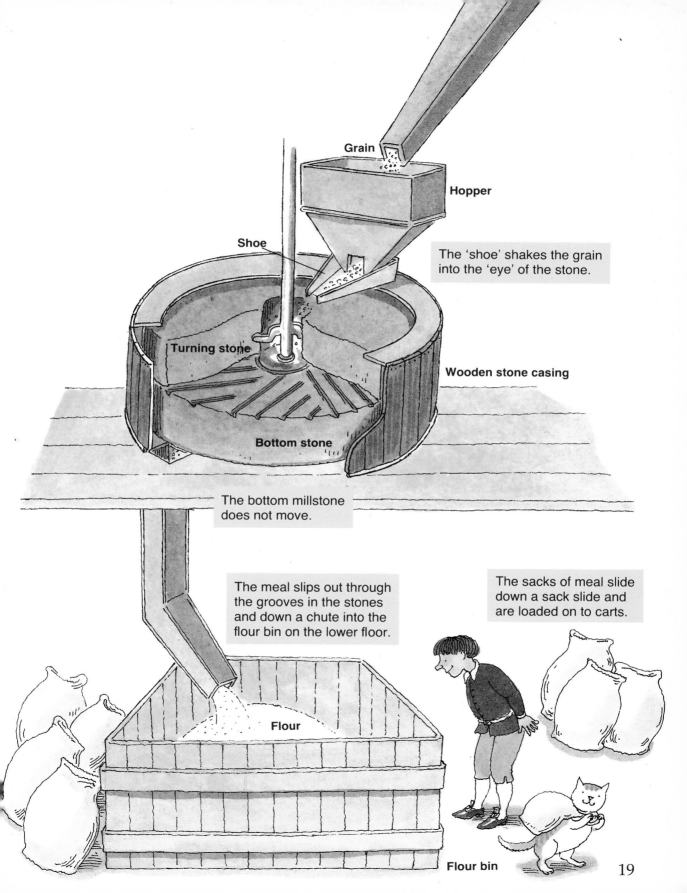

Grain

Hopper

Shoe

The 'shoe' shakes the grain into the 'eye' of the stone.

Turning stone

Wooden stone casing

Bottom stone

The bottom millstone does not move.

The meal slips out through the grooves in the stones and down a chute into the flour bin on the lower floor.

The sacks of meal slide down a sack slide and are loaded on to carts.

Flour

Flour bin

19

Millstones

The later, taller mills had up to eight pairs of millstones, and older mills were often extended to fit in more millstones. Large pieces of the very hard stone needed to grind the finest flour were difficult to find and therefore expensive. Some millstones were made from pieces of stone cemented together and bound with an iron band. Cheaper, softer stone was used for grinding lower quality flour and cattle food. Mills were also used for grinding pepper, mustard, chalk for making whitewash and bones for making soap and fertilizers.

The grooves in the stones wore down quickly and often needed recutting. This was called 'dressing the stone'.

Deep grooves cut into the surface of a millstone.

Stone-dressers travelled from mill to mill, recutting stones with their wedge-shaped 'mill bills' made from tough carbon steel.

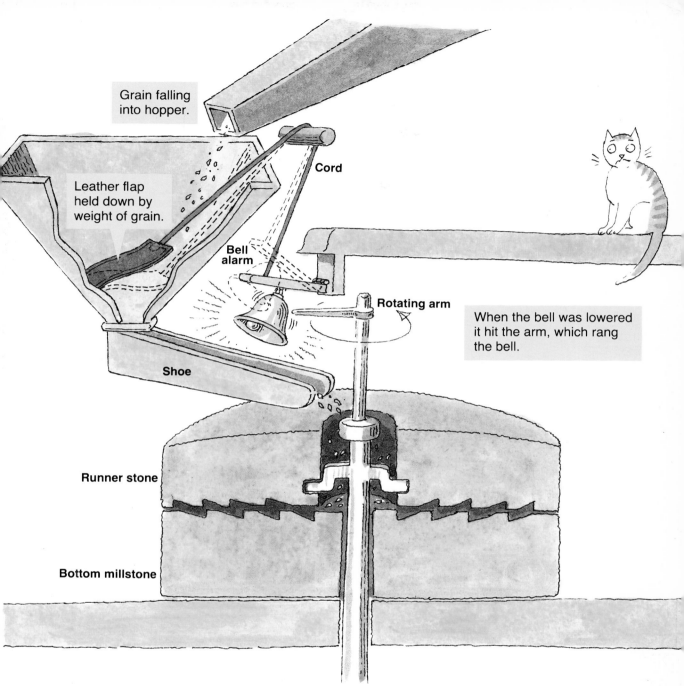

Grain falling into hopper.

Leather flap held down by weight of grain.

Cord

Bell alarm

Rotating arm

When the bell was lowered it hit the arm, which rang the bell.

Shoe

Runner stone

Bottom millstone

If the millstones turned when there was no grain between them, they rubbed together. This damaged the stones and made sparks which sometimes set mills on fire. To stop this from happening, a 'bell alarm' was fitted to the grain bins. A leather flap near the bottom of the hopper was attached by a cord to a bell. The weight of the grain held the leather down and kept the cord taut. When the grain ran low, the flap rose and the cord slackened, lowering the bell. A rotating arm then hit the bell, making it ring.

21

The governor

It was not possible to control the speed of the millstones as this depended on the strength of the wind. When the amount of grain reaching the stones increased, it tried to force the stones further apart, letting coarser flour fall through them. To keep the gap constant, the 'governor' was invented.

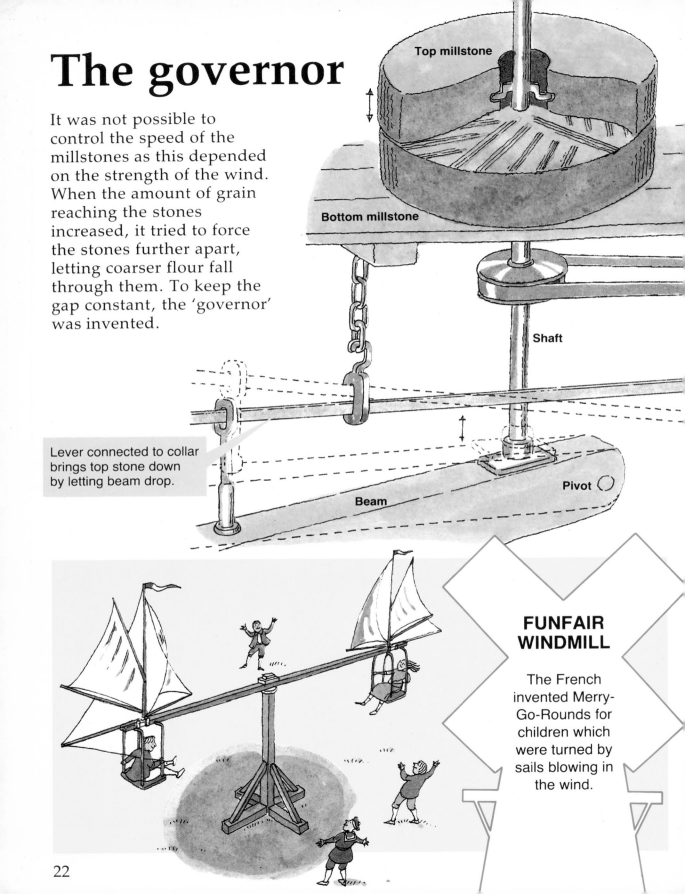

Top millstone

Bottom millstone

Shaft

Lever connected to collar brings top stone down by letting beam drop.

Beam

Pivot

FUNFAIR WINDMILL

The French invented Merry-Go-Rounds for children which were turned by sails blowing in the wind.

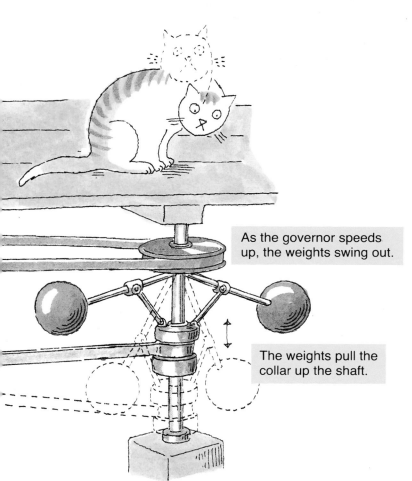

As the governor speeds up, the weights swing out.

The weights pull the collar up the shaft.

The lead weights on the spinning governor swung out if the speed of the runner stone increased. The weights were connected to a collar round the shaft and as they swung out, they pushed the collar up the shaft. The collar was connected to a lever and beam which, in turn, pulled down on the turning stone to stop the gap between the millstones from increasing.

As the wind dropped and the speed of the stone decreased, the weights fell and the beam pushed up on the stone to keep the gap from getting too small again.

When the mill speeds up in stronger winds, more grain falls between the stones. The governor stops the stones from being forced too far apart by this extra grain.

The chairs on a fairground roundabout swing outwards as the speed increases, like the lead weights on the governor.

Sieving the flour

The 'flour' produced in the early mills was gritty and full of chaff and other bits and pieces. The baker had to sift it by hand. Later, ways to clean and grade the flour using wind power were developed.

Bellows powered by the mill puffed air over the meal to separate the lighter chaff from the heavier grains of flour. This was then shaken through a coarse sieve to remove the gravel and other bits of rubbish. It then went into a rotating cloth drum called a bolter. The tube of cloth sagged from the weight of the flour and the bulge rubbed against wooden bars around the bolter, brushing the flour off the cloth.

Usually the bolter had three sections of cloth sieve, closer weaves giving fine flour and coarser weaves letting through the bigger grains of flour. At first, calico was used to sieve the flour. Later, strengthened silk produced even finer flour.

By the 18th century, mills could produce the fine white flour demanded by rich people. The wholewheat flour produced now for the health food market would have been considered second-best at that time.

Flour chute

The first sieve shook the fine white flour out.

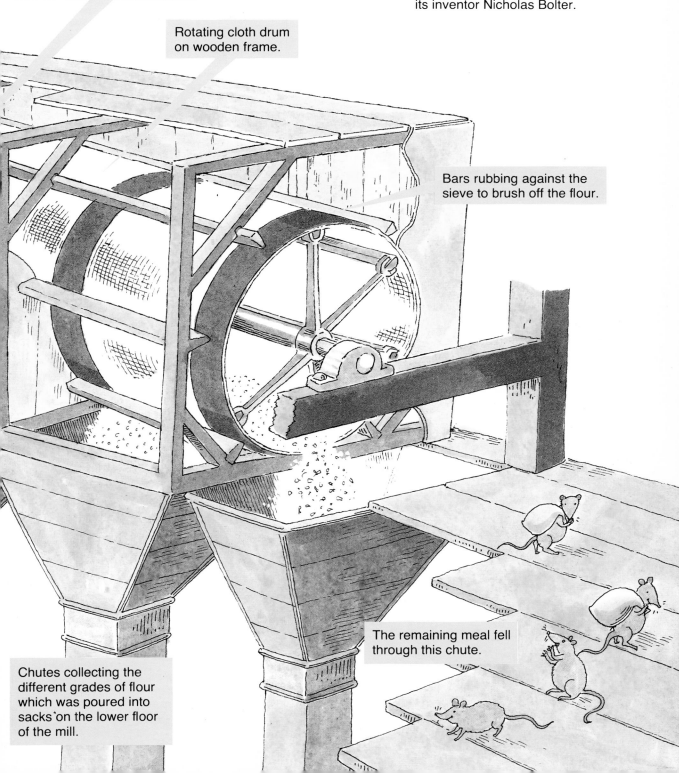

The second sieve shook the wholemeal flour out, leaving the bran to be shaken out of the final sieve.

The bolter was named after its inventor Nicholas Bolter.

Rotating cloth drum on wooden frame.

Bars rubbing against the sieve to brush off the flour.

The remaining meal fell through this chute.

Chutes collecting the different grades of flour which was poured into sacks on the lower floor of the mill.

Building materials

When someone wanted to build a mill, they probably visited other mills in the area to get ideas for the design. The engineer and carpenter employed to do the work may have already worked on other mills, but as there was no mass production of machinery, each mill was designed and built individually. Although the problems were the same in all mills, the design of the equipment inside the mill varied, partly depending on the space available.

Over the years, mills were altered and added too and new equipment was being designed all the time, both to make the miller's life easier and to improve the quality of the flour.

In early mills, almost all the machinery was made of wood. The gear wheels were made of wood and the cogs were wooden pegs fitted into the wheels. The shafts were usually made from oak wood. The gear wheels and cog pegs were often made of apple or pear wood, because it was very hard wearing.

As villages grew, some wooden post and smock mills had to be moved to new sites. First the machinery would be moved, then the body of the mill was moved on a sledge or rollers towed by up to a dozen horses or oxen.

They're moving the mill.

Slowly does it.

Later, much of the machinery was made of iron. When a wooden part wore out, it was often replaced by an iron piece, leaving the rest still in wood. The complicated cog shapes were cast in iron. Some millers still preferred the old wooden machinery, which was much quieter to run and easier to repair. For instance, a broken cast iron wheel would probably have to be replaced, but a wooden wheel could usually be repaired.

Gear wheels made partly of cast iron and partly of beech wood.

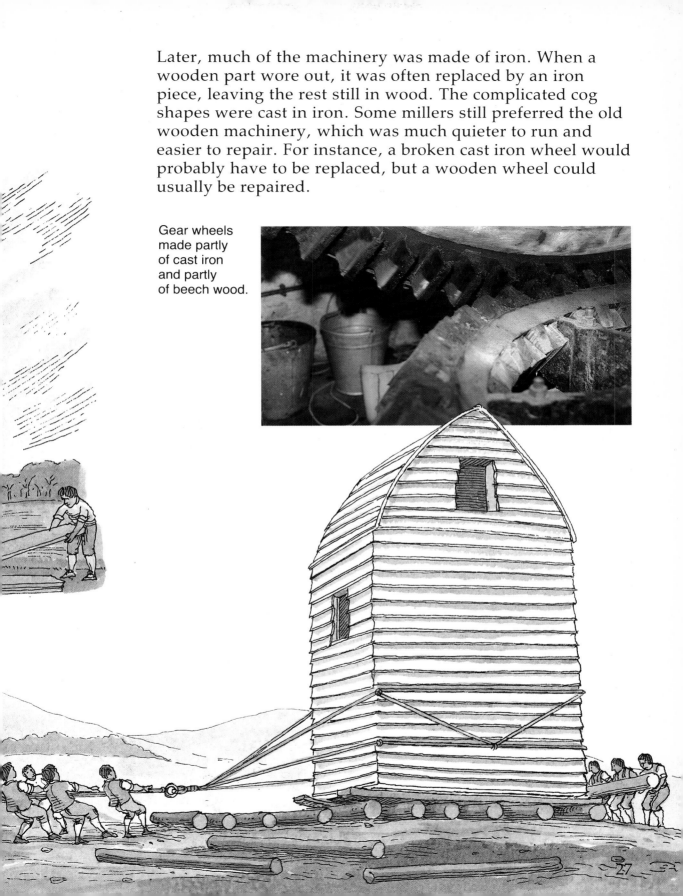

Drainage mills

In the low-lying English fens and flat parts of Holland, mills were built to drain land which was under water so that it could be used for farming. Drainage mills had sails which were connected by a shaft and gears to a scoop wheel. When this wheel turned, it scooped up the water from a drainage ditch and poured it into a higher level river or drain.

As less machinery was needed in a drainage mill, there was room for the miller and his family to live in the larger mills. The mill was often surrounded by water and could only be reached by boat.

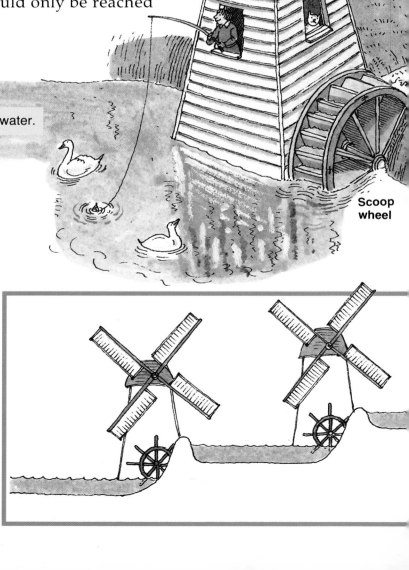

Low-lying land under water.

Scoop wheel

By the 19th Century, steam pumps were being used for drainage and the use of windmills gradually stopped. Some drainage mills were converted to grind corn instead. Even after the invention of steam engines, which burnt coal, people went on using windmills to save the cost of buying new engines. Many windmills were still being used at the beginning of this century. Smaller windpumps continue to be used to pump water.

28

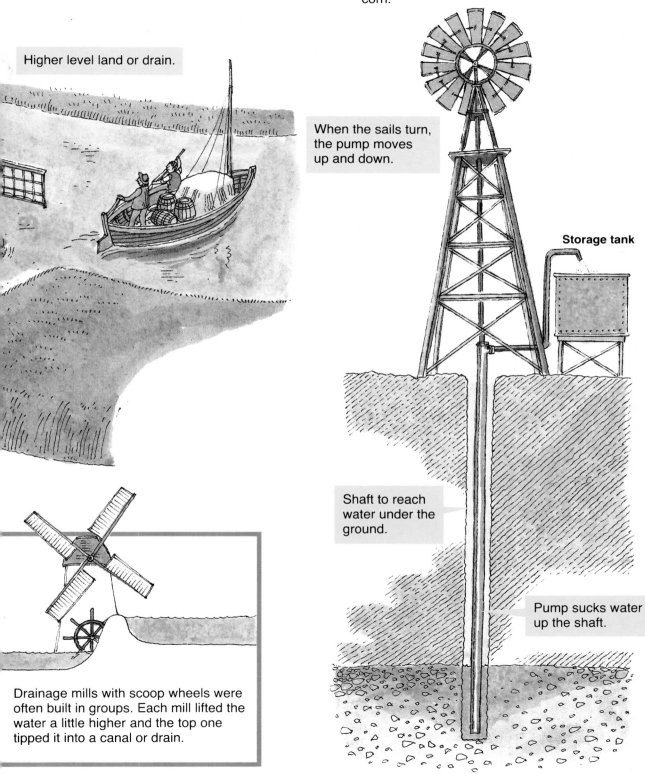

This American windmill was used for pumping water. Larger versions were built for grinding corn.

Higher level land or drain.

When the sails turn, the pump moves up and down.

Storage tank

Shaft to reach water under the ground.

Pump sucks water up the shaft.

Drainage mills with scoop wheels were often built in groups. Each mill lifted the water a little higher and the top one tipped it into a canal or drain.

Wind power

Wind power doesn't pollute the atmosphere like power stations which burn coal or oil, and people are now using wind turbines to generate electricity. Tiny wind turbines charge batteries to run televisions and lighting on boats and caravans. They also produce electricity for buildings in remote areas.

Where there is enough land and strong winds, wind 'farms' with as many as two hundred giant windmills can be built. Before deciding on a site, engineers put up a tall mast with equipment to measure the speed of the wind at different heights and at different times of the year. They can then decide on the best height for the wind turbines and make sure they will generate enough electricity to be worthwhile.

Phew, it's getting warm in here!

FLYING WINDMILLS

In the 1920s, small windmills were used to generate electricity and warm pilots' flying suits. But when the windmills turned too fast, the flying suits overheated!

30

Capturing wind energy on wind farms like this one does not harm the environment. In the future, wind energy will probably be an important source of energy throughout the world.

Look, it's a forest of windmills!

They're big aren't they?

The modern wind turbine is a giant propeller with two or three solid blades, instead of sails, at the top of a tower. The blades may be vertical or horizontal and are connected through a gearbox to an electric generator. The windshaft and brake wheel are made of very strong steel and the great spur wheel is much more complicated and runs hundreds of times as fast as the same wheel in old windmills.

Some people are against the idea of wind farms. They think wind turbines are ugly and noisy. The same complaints were probably made about windmills when they were first built, towards the end of the 12th century.

This British wind turbine produces enough power for about 600 homes. About 20 per cent of Britain's energy could be produced from the wind.

Index